I0148620

The Intimacy of Spoons

poems

Praise for *The Intimacy of Spoons: Poems* by Jim Minick

If you had to pick just one utensil from the kitchen drawer, just one piece of cutlery as tool and weapon, most of us, no doubt, would reach for the fork or knife. Both are defined by their sharpness, both can tear and cut and stab. But Jim Minick turns away from all that and in his hand wields a spoon . . . Yes, a spoon—lowly and simple and dull—an implement whose usefulness is an act of holding, whose power is steadfast tenderness. And this collection—*The Intimacy of Spoons*—is a result of making that choice time and again, each poem showing just how the worst of what we face today—be the climate crisis or our aging bodies or our distracted, grief-stricken lives—can be fought with the weapon of empathy and grace. The result then is a book filled with dogs and birds and deep attention, each poem a spoonful of medicine to administer healing to our broken world.

—Nickole Brown, author of *To Those Who Were Our First Gods*

Jim Minick declaims, "This is how the Earth sings," and in his poems he works out a kind of peace, a form of grace, informed by a deep and loving knowledge of place, tended to with compassion and praise and a cleareyed gaze that lets nothing escape. He offers up the sound a coyote makes, explains our kinship with oak and elm, claiming this world is enough, if we'd only care for it.

—Todd Davis, author of *Coffin Honey* and *Native Species*

Throughout this collection, Jim Minick's own bright song traces the tender fascination he has sustained for various winged creatures over his lifetime—what they have gifted him by association, what he has learned from them, and the pleasure he has taken in rapt observation. Glimpses of mortality, ecological precarity, and Minick's many encounters with birds take us deep into a landscape of the heart with a mature poet who grieves extinction, damage, and destruction, as much as he celebrates his love for feathered creatures and their persistent songs.

At the heart of this accessible and skillful collection, readers will appreciate Minick's love of his wife, earth wisdom, and of course birds, while he grapples with how humankind has emptied the garden not just of themselves, in the myth of Eden, but of many other possibilities through forms of careless self-indulgence that have proven reckless for our entire ecosystem. In the rousing and ironic "Mal and Slick's Ballad," Minick drills into the dangerous place of religion in all this damage we've wrought on a quest for heaven. Jim Minick is a poet who can range from high to low rhetoric, employing formal grace or friction, always with clarity of purpose and characteristic honesty of expression. *The Intimacy of Spoons* is a collection to read and reread to unlock its treasures.

—Cathryn Hankla, author of *Lost Places: On Losing and Finding Home*

With a near-boundless affection for the overlooked and quotidian, *The Intimacy of Spoons* reminds us that we are surrounded by the miraculous if we but choose to notice it. From the way he recounts the small kindness of rescuing a cardinal to the philosophical depth he finds in considering the common teaspoon, it's clear Jim Minick is a poet of generosity and kindness. By turns wistful, whimsical, and wise, this is a book I'll be rereading for a long time to come. It's a delight.

—Doug Van Gundy, author of *A Charm Against Forgetting*

Here is a book that opens the kitchen drawer and finds a "mirror that fogs with breath" among the ladles. *The Intimacy of Spoons* shines its light into a "world made bright / by a creature who / knows dark." In these poems, Mortality is the name of a dog who will lick your face and the Fix-It Man tells of the double murder of his parents. Looking hard at logged land, Minick speaks tenderly of shade. Listening to the rain "with one ear," he extends a hand to those who want to find their "way back into the earth."

—Amy Wright, author of *Paper Concert*

Also by Jim Minick:

Fiction
  Fire Is Your Water

Nonfiction
  The Blueberry Years: A Memoir of Farm and Family
  Finding a Clear Patch
  Without Warning: The Tornado of Udall, Kansas

Poetry
  Her Secret Song
  Burning Heaven

Edited
  All There Is to Keep by Rita Riddle

The Intimacy of Spoons

poems

Jim Minick

MADVILLE
PUBLISHING

LAKE DALLAS, TEXAS

Copyright © 2024 by Jim Minick
All rights reserved
Printed in the United States of America

FIRST EDITION

Requests for permission to reprint or reuse material from this work
should be sent to:

Permissions
Madville Publishing
PO Box 358
Lake Dallas, TX 75065

Cover Art & Design: Suzanne Stryk
Author Photo: Pam Campbell

ISBN: 978-1-956440-75-1 paperback
978-1-956440-76-8 ebook
Library of Congress Control Number: 2023946208

For Sarah

Contents

*

1   To Spoon

3   Coyote Grace

4   James and Jim Ponder Enough

6   First Hard Frost

7   Sighs

8   Lasts

10   What If We Learn at Last, but the Land Stops Forgiving?

12   One Apple Blossom

13   Vessel

14   Every Person Deserves a Statue and Every Statue Deserves
     a Sledgehammer

16   Good Dirt

17   Stress Test

21   Spoon Riddle

22   Because in the Village of Where

23   Diminished

24   Whale Light

26   Still Dark

27   Trenched

28   Mort for Short

29   Wrestling the Dead

31   Exercise

33   Ode to a Basket

34   Know the Trees, One by One

**

37   Elegy for My Body

***

51   Another Truth
52   To Spoon the Dark
53   Why Birds?
55   Spangled
56   The Collar
57   Tim Slack, the Fix-It Man
58   A Boat Called *Kinfolks*
59   Gas
62   Spoonbill
63   A Spoon Against Forgetting
64   To Thumbnail Evolving
65   What Happens to Bulldozers in Heaven
66   Earth Diving
67   Mal and Slick's Ballad
70   Hawk Says Finally
71   When You Realize the Future
72   Lincoln's Ax
74   The Oldest Spoon
75   Broken Wing
77   Cup of Sun
78   Gluteal Fold
79   Blink
81   The Intimacy of Spoons

82   Acknowledgments
84   About the Author

*

To Spoon

To spoon is not to fork—
that's what we do to steaks
and roads and manure.

To fork is to pierce, penetrate, puncture.
To fork is to split and branch,
to pay up and cough out,

but also to tune.
We forklift crates. We pitchfork hay.
The devil never carries a spoon.

Can you bang forks and get a song?

To spoon is not to knife—
that's what we do too often
to bodies and silence.

To knife is to slice,
to stab and wound,
to skin, filet, and butcher.

To knife is to dam
water that once
spooned the land.

Can you play knives without getting hurt?

Yet the tool is innocent:
a fork feeds or gigs;
a spoon ladles soup or cooks H—

and a knife? To scalp
and to scalpel
both require a sharp blade.

Listen to the drumming of the spoons.

To spoon is to slip into sleep
and the same soft, slow breath,

to listen to the rain
with one ear.

Coyote Grace

From low in her belly, a coyote lifts
her voice to ascend that organ pipe
of a throat to clarity of dusk
and cue for pups to join with yips and squeaks
that nurture the air to vibrate
with what seems like joy like ecstasy
of sound of the body an instrument
the larynx a box to strum with one long exhale—
this yodeling school for pups, choir
practice with only sopranos, for now,
and time to learn to listen to kin
on haunches nearby and a mile away:
this nightly hairy news with lips wide,
eyes bright, whiskers funneling the wind,
this town-square opera of hot breath,
hillside tail-curled revival—
O for a Thousand Tongues to Sing?—
jazzed with ostinatos and skat
for non-cats, fresh blood overture,
roadkill serenade, growling gratitude,
a thick-fur kind of grace, close
enough to hollow out your chest, close enough
to hear each voice, close enough to sing
along and then listen to the ache
of an echo long and slow and longer still.

It ends as sudden as it starts,
no benediction, no *amen*,
unless the whole song is one long
amen to this holy, falling dark.

And then we eat.

James and Jim Ponder Enough

we live inside a hollow full of oaks and elms
that hold the light in a columned quiet space—

a hollow full of wind-song and bird-caught clouds
and the barred owl's echoing questions

stay the chestnut doe whispers
to her fawn shy and pied

star-speckled salamanders slick banks
wide-mouthed orchids drop to kiss moss

once a bear wintered here in the dark of a log
soft snores becoming morning frost on the rim

in the very bottom this cup of land holds
a seep a muddy ooze a spring too small to sing

remember water carved this hollow
to bear it back on the backs of bears

it is enough this touch of oak this comfort
of elm this holy kinship enough

we live inside a hollow full of spokes and realms
of no light the quiet not quiet the space

full of fog and one crow call loud
to blanket another snuffed-out question

steal away we whispered
as our father died

slick cheeked we gave thanks
he didn't know any more loss

his eyes darkened each pupil a hollow log
breath slowed the cold crept down each limb

valleys crowfoot thick around eyes—each fold
draining the blue to gray to nothing

so cup what color remains before it flows
and know he came back for one last stare

is it enough, this memory? and this fort
of trees, this home—is it really enough?

First Hard Frost

and the bear's fur glistens and rolls,
the fawn grows fat on wormy apples,
the bluestem glitters, seed dispersed.

Each crystal-covered, mitered blade
bends the light to flicker and shade.

First hard frost and the goldenrod
no longer brightens the speckled air,
wands of aster emptied of purple pulse—

both now beheaded and brown,
their roots live on underground.

First hard frost and the sunrise sparks
yellow hickories, blazing oaks,
the wine-red creeper vine that climbs,

waving in warblers to settle and sup
this blood of the earth slowly drawn up.

So tell me why, in all of this,
am I so afraid of Death's quick kiss?

Sighs

How they wallop with softness,
how they soothe with the slow rush
of wind through the forest in your dog's nose,
each follicle a pine to sing a contented song
of nothing-could-be-better,
of home-is-sweet-and-here-and-now—

That's Ray, the King of Sighs—
as he naps, I pet his ears and feel
their coolness and so lay a blanket
over his big-boned body, his thin tan fur—
the tucking in elicits that quick inhale,
that slow exhale of just-rightness;

or on movie nights, how he lies
big-bellied between us to knead
and chew his towel like a puppy
falling asleep with towel-filled mouth,
or just pausing to rest and sigh
and then knead some more;

or every night when I'm last in bed,
his family all settled, the dark
cave of our room quiet and safe—
from his pillow on the floor
he heaves that chest to sigh
a long and slow *yes.*

Not just Ray sighs like this.
This is how the Earth sings,
the bumble bee too,
how we all are meant to sigh
with each breath until the end:
Breathe in scent and light.
Breathe out wings and flight.

Lasts

i.
They arrive unannounced—
>last kiss and welcome home hug
>last hiccup and "hurry up"
>last horse snort and nicker;

and all the time and every time—
>last catbird feather gray in hand
>last dimpled blueberry on lips
>last puppy wiggle and lick;

we rush through them unaware—
>last bloom of chestnut
>last bare-leafed ash
>last ice-cloaked hemlock;

our lasts trampling all over this blue marble.

ii.
Juncos: slate-black against snow
in winter, white bellies among snow-
drops in spring. They never sing
until they're gone
to their tundra home
for the summer,
and they never let you know
when they part.
Goodbye, I always say too late.

iii.
And what about those other lasts?
I have saved beechnut trees
and acorn-loaded oaks,
foods they loved;
I've waited for flocks

of passenger pigeons
to blacken the sky for days
once more. And a parakeet
in these woods—so hard
to imagine, so hard to not
look for that splash of green and red.
Goodbye, we always say too late,
or we never get a chance to say at all.

iv.
Twenty years ago, monarch butterflies
glided these fields thistle to thistle
too many to count;
now they are too few.
I save milkweed, look for eggs,
but what will remain
twenty years from now?
Goodbye doesn't have to be
the only way to say love.

What If We Learn at Last, but the Land Stops Forgiving?

To the men who logged this land in 1965
leaving tire ruts clogged with leaves & scarred oaks hollow &
now tall arching over skid trails, green alleys I hike
pressing down with each step the already compacted
soil that a lifetime later still grows nothing—for all,
thank you.

      To the men who logged this land when they came home
from the war, the civil one, to find old growth so ripe
it took a day to fell just one—red, white & black oak,
poplar, maple, chestnut, walnut & slippery elm.
You milled each massive trunk here by the creek, bog too soft,
so you built a timber-bridge of chestnut culls & left
slab heaps, rail spikes & spindly logs below hillsides stumped
& suddenly empty. Rain lifted the powdered soil
& runneled it down to bury your debris in mud
so deep the wood purpled instead of rotted until
125 years later, we dug a pond,
uncovering logs salvaged into storied lumber—
thank you.

      To the men who quarried another hillside
in 1795, poor whites & poorer slaves
& bossmen yelling to dig for iron, for zinc, for
lead, for ore of any color. But you found none,
your horses exhausted, your shovels ringing empty.
Instead of mines, you left ravines thirty coffins deep
& bear-wallow pits & now two hundred years later,
white pines tower alongside, filling each slough needle
by needle, but still each trench is baren, still no soil—
still, thank you, all.

And to this dirt, who daily reminds
us what death tastes like & to these stumps, who sprout chestnut
wands to blight year after year & to this poplar we
gouged while building our road, who still offers us shade &
air, rain patter on leaves & forgiveness if we be-
gin to believe—for all this & more, thank you, thank you.

One Apple Blossom

opens in spiral,
petal by petal,
five pink-tinged scoops
of sun calling bees
with scent of sex. This
bloom swells to seed-dense,
juice-packed ovary,
and I kiss the tips
of what used to be
petals. Then I eat
this one apple
from bloom-end
in, unspiraling
the tender
blossom.

Vessel

for Kathryn and Karen on their wedding

From the furnace
the gaffer pulls

gathers of glass
melted and glowing.

She kisses pipe
and gently blows

coaxing a molten,
messy beauty.

Colors change
yet still express

the blue and green
of prairie grass.

Fire roars,
the gaffer twirls.

Fire shapes,
the gaffer waits.

Grains of sand
bubble and fuse

to curved windows
bending light.

This marriage—
breath and dreams

a vase to hold
the tender bloom

your new life.

Every Person Deserves a Statue and Every Statue Deserves a Sledgehammer

after watching Ghostbusters *and hearing about Heather Heyer in the same week*

The Twin Towers still stand,
and when two other buildings explode,
only fake rock hits the ground.
Everyone escapes.
No one has to jump.

And after the great eruption
of blimp-sized Mr. Stay Puft,
globs of gooey marshmallow
coat the city, the sidewalk, the people.
No dust. No ashes.
No one ever dies.

We were so foolish to believe ghosts
could be busted, to believe spirits lived
out there and not inside.

****

Statues are ghosts
turned into marble,
saints easy to hammer
with a sledge
unlike the real ghost

of Robert E.
with his once-brown eyes
and once-trimmed beard
sleeping under the stars
of the Confederate flag
all across the South
and North and East and West.

We will never bust that ghost.
He lives on in each of us

just like Booker T. & Malcolm X &
Zitkála-Šá,

just like Heather Heyer
gone to Charlottesville
to say Robert E. is no
greater or lesser than any of us,

to say, "If you're not outraged,
you're not paying attention,"

to ask, now that I too
am a ghost,
where is my statue?

****

And that song from the movie
that worms inside
to play on and on and on—
"Who ya gonna call?"—

I dialed the number,
the line is dead.

Good Dirt

Already I have tasted fire.
Tongue to tongue,
I have licked
its heat and flame,
smelled hair
singed in my nose.

Already I have heard
the pop of skin
after it blistered.
Such pain I did not know
until the nerves went numb
from the bright explosion.

Let me tell you:
Fire's deepest secret
is a heart that has no color,
and in that heart,
the rumble and roar
disappear.

When I die,
the tongues will lick me again,
only more fully
and only after my spirit
has already leapt.

Ashes from bone
make good dirt.

Stress Test

A phone call at the start
to slap me from sleep. Or

does it begin before,
when a gas explosion

scorched my arm and face?
Or before that with cells

colliding like flint and
steel to spark and grow? What

nucleus of stress em-
bedded in Y and X

to grow into that al-
most obliterating

pitch dark passage of birth?
Or did this stress begin

generations back with
blood of running and blood stopped?

Anyway, the call: *We need
more tests*, the voice explains,

so, of course, I say yes.
Next day I wait alone

with Gideon's black book
and *Wheel of Fortune* loud.

Then Nurse punctures skin to
plunge liquid into vein.

Nuclear isotopes,
she explains. *To get a*

better picture. We watch
the tiny Chernobyls

disappear. *They'll be gone*
in sixty hours, if you

drink lots of water. I
drink three cups and want more.

Next I lie to watch a space-
craft hover over chest

beaming my heart across
the galaxy of this room.

Don't move, Nurse warns before
she leaves. So I stifle

each cough, ignore all itches.
The machine hums and clicks.

Minutes become eons
until finally it stops.

I breathe and scratch and cough
and think of the four *s's*

in *stress test*, hissing snakes
of steam *ssss-ing* from valves.

No nuclear explosions,
yet. So I return to wait

in a place invented
by stress: cement compressed

to pounds per inch; glass from sand
burned clear; wood, wind-shaken,

rings curling a dark heart—
all must pass. Or else.

This is why I am here:
Once last month when I tried

to rest, my heart fluttered
like a wren and then slammed

the bone bars of my chest
for just a moment—

before it calmed, unlike
the panic in my head.

At last, Doc appears
while Nurse connects

electrodes and I tread
the rolling mill. *Your heart*

looks good, Doc says, then adds,
so far. Soon I'm huffing,

staring at a heart poster.
I ask how the blood moves.

Doc says, *This is the world's*
best pump, proud like he made it.

Man-made pumps are only
a third as good. He taps.

Oxygen-depleted blood
comes in here. His pen maps

blood from heart to lungs to
heart to brain. *A closed system,*

nothing better. I'm sweating
now and holding tight, steep

ground whirring underfoot.
Yet I get no closer

to that heart. I breathe hard,
watch the monitor with Doc.

This looks good, he nods. *Yours
went up real smooth, no hitch.*

I'm going to slow you down.
Soon I walk on flat ground.

The whirring dies. No more
hurry to go nowhere.

You're fine, Doc smiles. *No need
to invade this time.*

*A little arrhythmia,
a hiccup of the heart.*

At home, I hike the woods
to heave ax over and

over, my body a pump
that *thunks* each round of oak,

riving the heart to reveal
a salvation of sorts

and the slow truth of fire.

Spoon Riddle

Hang a spoon on your nose
and what do you get?
A mirror that fogs with breath.

Because in the Village of Where

Through the Village of Where
the Whodunits run and
Because always chases sly Why.

But Why never goes
to any old Where
without a wink and a When.

When and Who,
as only they can,
hold hands and jump from the bridge.

They wiggle their toes
and never let go
and plunge into dark, cold Time.

The bluegills and eels,
the Whatifs and Hows
nibble on When and Who.

Because just nods and
wishes them well
then turns to search for Why.

Diminished

in response to Robert Frost's "Ovenbird"

You said there was a singer everyone
had heard, a joke, I'm sure, even then,
a hundred years ago. But here's the jest
I have to use each time I teach your poem,
"No turkey here, no culinary test,
no, this bird's a winsome warbler who builds
a funny nest."

       When I was young, my home
had woods and ovenbirds galore that pealed
like hammers their "teacher" song in woods that live
no more. What happens to directives
like "in singing not to sing" when
forests fill with emptiness
and no bird's left to sing? Forgotten
implies memory, never the less.

Whale Light

after Paul Nicklen's photograph "Liquid Curtain" in Born to Ice

The fluke is no fluke—
this happens all the time,
these miracle windows
we never look through
except this once.

Whale surfaced.
Whale breathed.
And now Whale returns
to that other world,
the long arc of sleek body
ending with this—
not a tail
but a window
of water.

Made by velocity
and liquid pouring
over skin, the trailing
skim is stained
glass without the stain,
fragments of sky
oranged by the gone sun—
it too having dove back down
to that other world.

The water window is not
clear, has no mountains
or waves on the other side—
it is just light
with a frothy frame.

Already the liquid glass
is shattering back to sea.

What do we see
when we look through
whale light?
The world made bright
by a creature who
knows dark

but that dark isn't really
all dark or the only—
there are other windows
and other lights
for all to see.

Still Dark

From the sugarberry tree,
dove sings her low hello
cardinal his sharp cheer, cheer.

Wren rattles & darts & calls for tea,
while far away, chickadee repeats,
"I'm here, I'm here."

Such exuberance
before the sun
even rises,

such joy
I wish
I knew.

And in this moment,
I do,
I do.

Trenched

I always read about how cities empty the country
of people (especially the young)...& of wheat &
apples & celery & cheese & fish & hogs &
lambs & cows & hens...& of trees &
coal & gas & water &—if they could
—every bit of clean air.

Then I too left
for a better job
in the city
where I found
no silence
& little wildness
except in rotted
factories & still
no silence.
I felt
emptied
but also
filled.

I was trenched
like the mile-wide hollow
back home, a landfill becoming hill
filled with no land. Every hour tractor-trailers
transport their stench hundreds of miles from New York,
DC & Philly to dump diapers & sporks & so many disposables,
& then hurry back for more & more & more. That's what the city does to you.

Mort for Short

Mortality: The Disease.
Mortality: The Cure.
Mortality, the name
of my next dog
who will lick my face
and greet me at the door.

Wrestling the Dead

for Brian Ott (1963-2022)

In art class, Mrs. Cooper made us
preppies & stoners work side by side,
together, like staves in a barrel
learning difference disappears for a while.

And every day, Brian Ott walked in late,
red-eyed & smiling, to sit beside me,
shoving a little shoulder shove, taking little
seriously as he settled on the bench,

spilling supplies over the table,
saying, *Excuse me*, in a mocking voice.
Then he'd ask what I was listening to
which led to Led Zeppelin & trading LPs—

Edgar Winter free-riding to Frampton,
Aerosmith's sweet emotions raining on
Uriah Heep & Pink Floyd comfortably
numbing us back to Zeppelin in through the out door.

On the long bus rides to away matches,
those green seats cold & slick, we traded
punches, not the flat-fisted kind that don't hurt
much, but the one-knuckle-elevated

kind aimed at bicep sure to bruise. Before
each punch, Brian blew on his fist, rubbed it
on his chest like polishing a brass knuckle
for its special task. I was always first

to flinch, so he always won. Forty years
after graduation sundered us staves,
we wrestled again last night & despite
him being forty pounds lighter, he had

me on my back in an illegal hold
& he laughed in his devilment as I
thrashed & hit & kicked until I woke.

How can a ghost   still throw a punch   so full of love?

Exercise

for Stuart Dischell

Exercise
so
much
you
sweat
poems.

Then poems
will seize
and eat
through so
many yous
like matches

in a match-
book ignited, poems
blazing through you,
words that incise
like knives so
shiny sharp. Whet

them until the whet-
stone breaks and much
of nothing remains. So
you'll know your poems,
then, those shifty spies
who live inside you.

They'll give anything up, you
included. They thirst for sweat,
drink it like wine, exercise
their power until so much
is created, poems birthing poems,
you delirious with insomnia, sow-

ing droplet words to make rain so
the fires might fizzle and you
can sleep. *I want sleep, Poems!*
But I want you too, sweet
fire-eyed devils who know too much—
I sense how great your size.

So you say, *Maybe*, my pen sweat-
ing blue yous, my life a burnt match.
The poem played out, for now, exorcised.

Ode to a Basket

Two reeds to hold the shape
of your hands, two turning
to four turning to eight
turning to something to hold
the loneliness
I want to carry away
to bury or to burn.

A basket is never empty.

Hunger is another name
for basket. To market we journey
loaded with expectation,
our punnets filled with red
of pepper and strawberry,
red of Pontiac, red of desire.

A basket is never full.

This summer I cracked a rib,
and the basket of my body
turned fragile, the contents
unsure of its weavers and spokes.
To laugh hurt. To breathe
hurt. The ache at night
for your touch hurt.

If I weave
my fingers with yours,
we can hold
for a little while
that loneliness, that hurt.

Know the Trees, One by One

Know the trees, one by one,
rough-barked, smooth, shingled, or banded,
oak, hickory, maple, or gum.

Like a blind man walking, comb
the dimpled woods with feathery hands
'til you know the trees, one by one.

Like a deaf man singing, hone
your tongue so you unravel the stand
calling, "Oak, hickory, maple, gum."

What is time to a tree honeycombed
by bees? Rings retell the land
if you know the trees, one by one.

What is never to a bear that dens
in a tree, snoring in the dark hand
of oak, hickory, maple, or gum?

Kiss like lightning every cone.
Like a bobcat scratch your telegrams.
Know the trees, one by one.
Oak, hickory, maple, gum.

**

Elegy for My Body

i.

There is no *aid* in decade.
The word is a lie, should be *decayed*.
All the years pull your ears so you hear
      the *echo* in second
      the *ending* in pending

                  the *tic-tic-tic*
                  in Minick-ick-ick.

ii.

How many bodies have I buried?
How many?

iii.

Time is a bird
that flies by so fast—warping
space with speed, a raven
ravenous for the sun,
nevermoring my thumb
when I try to hitch a ride,
a bird that blurs the years
melting pocket watches
like Dali in his daily
practice of stretching
a canvas to bend
the ticking hand.

iv.

How many holes have I dug,
how much dirt have I tossed
onto the bodies
of dogs and kin and friends?

V.

You can't really *do* time;
it simply does us,
or undoes us,
us beings in the time being being beings
on Times Squared
waiting for the big ball to fall,
our Horror-scopes in *The Times*
saying Dickens was full of
lousy indecision and just like that (*snap your fingers*),
the big ball gets stuck halfway,
the new year suddenly on hold,
the crowd stunned by the witching
hour, the two-timing play-by-play announcer
calling for replays as we shift
to a TV-time-out and more
million-dollar, sixty-second spots
for munchie madness specials
like new square dates
picked from the old calendar tree,
those sweet fruits we let slip-
knot down our throats
while our heart's tick-tocker
swings like that stuck ball
on an ever-slowing pendulum
just hang-timing there
waiting to
drop.

vi.

How many bodies have I buried
in me? The deer and cows, the fish and birds.
How many berries and blood-red beets?

vii.

By the way, what's your hourly rate?
Mine's an elbow that cuckoos on the half,
knuckles swollen with every full moon,
tides of tears that ebb and flow,
skin slashed with not-yet-pickled scars,
teeth that took a time-share
and ran away with their wisdom,
a heart full of the daily turn of burns and boils.
Stars used to twinkle light-years in my eyes.
At least the sky of my cheeks no longer sparkles
with a constellation of zits.
Over the hilly years, I have broken every hour-
glass to watch the sands of time wash out to sea,
and I've lived eras upon eras of errors
pigeon-toeing for so damn long
my knees are fucked
down, not up,
my back, too,
this slouching into bedlam
we call the fool-ness of time.

viii.

Oh, the infinity of emails,
the minutes of meetings,
the dry guts of grants,
the bullets of vitas—
all of it a slow burial
no matter how often or if
you ever ask how many.

ix.

What if we time-traveled to a place
that had no timelines or deadlines,
a No-Time Zone where watches had no hands,
they just stared blank-eyed,
and every hour was happy
no matter the drink,
and rush hour meant whatever juiced us—
jazz riffs or river trips,
horse rides or dog licks.

Then time times time would equal infinity,
the circle really unbroken
just pinched by
that bow-tied god,
and this tiny instant would be what it is—
an out-of-time unclipped whispered song called:
(*pause-breath*)   Now.

All the time in the world.

X.

How many nights have I missed
that black sheet of paper
white-perioded by stars?
Burial by pixel
one swipe at a time.

xi.

Gravity's laughing, always laughing,
as you march-time into a grave-time
tilling in the meantime's soil,
and until-ing it, too.
"Take your time," Ms. Gravity shouts,
dirt in her mouth. "There's time enough
and then some to call the taker-
under, make derangements,
cold chisel your name in stone,
choose your appalled bearers,
and order your velvet-lined, triple-walled, bronze-plated vault."
Ms. Gravity hands you her card and a shovel.
"Say hello to the worms for me," she snickers.
Then off she slinks to spray paint
on every mausoleum wall and bathroom stall:
For a good time, call x-x-x!
You can't help but call, each part of you
dialing—your belly, your biceps, your brain.
The tricks are never timeless,
and you can never hang up.

"Don't call!" I want to gallop across
the universe yelling to everyone.
"Put that quarter back in your pocket,
spend your time-coins elsewhere."
But we're born into a just-in-time world
where the pilot says, *Our ground time here
will be brief,* and there are no more
payphones and no more free time,
so we grind time
in our teeth as we sleep
with the nightlight flickering,
and it's too late.
It's always too late.

xii.

Trees are never late,
never early,
never really on time either—
"I'm in time," each one sings
as they hold the undreadful
wind and rain
and all that earth and light,
even the lightning
that might sunder them apart.

So I say
ROOTS!
Give me roots—
who cares how many—
I want them all:
oak and
elm, slippery with ease,
hickory and
maple, sap full of sugar—

Oh, let there be
hundreds,
billions,
so many roots—

let them burrow
into my body,
let them bury me
into
the sky
with leaves.

***

Another Truth

Last dusk of winter
the sky blown clear
to silhouette black oaks,
their branches lashes
to close on the blue eye of day.

Thoreau was wrong
to focus just on dawn.
To wake to an infinite
expectation of dusk
is also another way.

To Spoon the Dark

Yesterday when we fought—
               the knife-slice of *no* so easy—
that moment we stared
               into each other's raw hurt,
I felt that black pit open
               and yaw me in.

               How do we live with such darkness?

Before the aural flower
               the wood thrush sings
in the gray dawn waking
               that eclipses the night,
he must trust the light
               will come.

               How does the darkness live with us?

And to make the flower
               the wood thrush sings,
he first must cup
               each note in his throat,
shape it with breath—
               those tiny lungs
must spoon the dark.

               Every seed, every song comes through the dark.

Those spoons we call our lungs

               can only hold so much.

Even this breath

               has to let go.

Why Birds?

Their songs, their brilliance,
their intricate nests and abundant curiosities.

Their dawn chorus calling
us to feel breath cross chords
and know the need to wake
the sun with song.

How they make me remember—
the sound of the gone ivory-billed
I learned from listening to LPs
with my grandfather;

or my first bluebird, its soft song
leading me to a hollow post
filled with four blue eggs—
something so startling and secret;

or the pileated that flew across
a country road at eye-level,
and we not yet married
and you yanking the wheel
back across the yellow line
as we crested a hill.

You knew then I was mad
with love for you and for birds
and you still said yes, and now,
over thirty years later, we're still
in love and even this evening
you pointed to the pileated
that cackled and flapped by our window.

Birds fly me away
from me, but also back—
the titmouse whistling
his simple call, two clear notes
echoing through the woods,
answering my poor reply,
saying hello,
flying me to you.

Spangled

Solstice. The sun stops to rest before the turning
back, while summer ticks along in the sweet practice
of sweat and flying flowers—azures and swallowtails,
sulfurs, skippers and nymphs, but no monarchs—that crown
is gone, pushed into a silent, star-studded night.
So I celebrate the Great Spangled Fritillary,
orange wings speckled with diamonds framed by rust.
One flies fast toward me and my sunflower-bright
shirt to light gentle on my chest, but when I look,
no butterfly tongue-taps the yellow cotton bloom
or sups salty skin. Fritillary flew through me.
What does it mean to have a butterfly inside?

The Collar

More than its beak that daggers the suet,
more than its whispers or squawks or pointed
crown, more than even the soft back
that looks like fur, not feathers,
gray fading to blue down the spine,
more than anything else, the blue jay
is defined by its collar, so black—
a lawyer's without the tie,
a queen's tight monarchy of the sky,
a priest's without the sanctity,
where a nest found is a nest eaten.

Or the collar could be this: a noose
that knots at the top of the head, burn
marks from a rope, a mythological
scar for some unknown crime, history
worn as jewelry, a stunning reminder
of our own mad and ugly past.

Tim Slack, the Fix-It Man

Been nothing but fans this week. This makes the fourth.
Had to replace an attic fan a day ago.
Lost five pounds doing that. Can't live
without a bathroom fan, can you?
(He has the old one out, dust caked thick.
It whirs in his hands, loud and rattling.) Yep,
it's bad. Sounds like a high-pitched
machine gun, don't it? Right there. (He points
to where it broke.)
                You say you're from Virginia?
That's where I grew up. Fauquier County,
The Plains. You hear about the double murder
last spring? Well, that was my parents,
the ones that got killed. Yep.
Fellow done it, I grew up with, lived
up the road. Needed money for drugs.
Tied them up and beat them with a bat.
Next day, they missed church. That's how
they got found.
             First double murder
in the state in twenty-five years.

Hit that switch, will you?

A Boat Called *Kinfolks*

for Gurney Norman

The Whole Earth got the Urge,
thanks to you, Divine-Gurney-Wilgus,
and we all headed East, not West,
to make a homestead out of stripped land.

And on our way, when we hitchhiked
some county road and Fat Monroe picked us up,
well, you taught us:
Don't chew his cigar
and definitely don't *Back Talk*
because like it or not he'll put
New Words to those *Old Wounds*,
and old words to those new wounds, too.

Oh Great Divine-Gurney-Wilgus, you midwifed
a whole country
named *Affrilachia*
and uncled generations of writers
who jump on *Trampolines* and eat blueberries.

Uncle G, your life has been a big-hearted hug
to these mountains and rivers.
You steady the boat called *Kinfolks*,
invite us aboard,
hand us an oar,
and shove off
on this river named *Ancient Creek*.
It's an *American Vein*
that will take us home
again and again and again.

Gas

for the boat-tailed grackles at Love's Truck Stop off I-95 near Brunswick, GA,
and for the woman on the bench in Jacksonville, FL

The boat-tailed grackle golden-eyes me
from the #8. He puffs his throat,
raises his crown, rudders his black tail.
Below, the magic mouth quick kisses
my credit card (petro-based plastic,
no doubt) & I pump gas, breathe fumes,
listen to the Stones sing, *It's a gas*,
all the while I'm occupied with time
& distance & their obliteration

& with the woman last night sleeping
outside on a bench, shouting, "Hey, mister,
you got food?" her back to me, yet turned
eyes white in lamp light—how had she known?
I walked on like the rest. Even the cop—
the old fart with crossed arms—ignored her.
"Hey, mister," again that voice a cliff,
an edge, a jump. I carried a clam-
shell of leftover curry (Massaman
with potatoes & onions & peanuts
& tofu & just the right hotness).
It glowed white in the dark. I was al-
most past her (elbow propped, blanketed
feet). "Hey, mister. I'm hungry."

                        I turned.
"Do you like hot food?" Her face confused.
"You know, spicy food?" Like that mattered.
"My mother's got a red bird pecking
at her medical bills." (Gray hair, knit
cap, wrinkles like me. Her mother? Still
alive?) The curry warmed her palm.
I hoped she had a spoon.

                                        Back at Love's
#8, boat-tailed grackle returns.
Another lands on shit-stained sprinkler
& I think why not eat lunch right here
with the boom of traffic, the thick fumes,
hunger's obliteration minutes away.

So I eat my PB & blackstrap.
Golden-eye screeches his ascending
screech, his feathers all shine & sine wave
iridescent as the spilled diesel
& the cellophane wrapper scratching
the chorded concrete like a guitar pick—
Jumpin' Jack Flash, it's a gas, gas, gas!

Mrs. Grackle with her brown head strides
'round the corner of the car—she too
golden-eyed & erect & I wonder
about that other gas, that other
cure for the homeless & unwanted.
What birds eyed those prisoners as they
entered Dachau, Belzec, and Auschwitz—
pigeons, maybe, or crows? How did they
navigate that dust-clotted sky?

And what birds will still be here to watch
the last drop of this gas? Grackles, maybe,
though they nest in saltmarshes soon gone
to flood. Or Eurasian collared doves
that bob & coo from guardrail, black neck-
laces on backward.

                    The grackles keep
beseeching, *Hey, mister, hey, mister.*
And like Mick, big lips kissing his mic,
I frown at the crumbs of a crust of bread—
why not share just a bite—that's what they

golden-eye, not me. So I break crust
& toss. Third try he dives & catches.
The others chase him to the Love's sign.

Why not embrace all that is ugly
& holy & here—the grackle's song
that isn't a song, a breadcrumb dropped,
the shiny ribbon of gasoline
that will get me closer to home.

But it's all right now, in fact, it's a

Spoonbill

i.
The spoon of the bill
acts like a filter,
a trap to catch small
creatures whose shells
give feathers color—
roseate, scorching pink,
orange on the tail—
shrimp resurrected
to shining brilliance
rising each morning
to stoke sullen air
with flames.

ii.
Love of a feather—
pink & soft & long,
bristly blue & sharp—
killed millions of birds:
spoonbills & crossbills,
flamingos & auks
upholstering hats
for derbies, the dead,
demure debutants.

iii.
Do birds know the way
to forgive like they
navigate the stars?
Can they long-legged
wade muddy waters
of love's hurts & needs?
Surely spoonbill so
bright knows love
& how to forgive.

A Spoon Against Forgetting

To canoe is to stroke
with a wooden spoon
what holds us
or what pulls us down.

To Thumbnail Evolving

When deer bone slipped and the hatchet
split you open to blood and meat
and nerves all linked to lungs heaved out
my throat by sound of animal
I knew suddenly as wild me,
thank you for protecting that nib
of bone, for the tip I can flip
for "all good" or to catch a ride,
thank you for the tap of this space
bar I can still drum with both thumbs
and not just one.

What Happens to Bulldozers in Heaven

Again, the neighbors didn't pick up
the bike, the truck, the scooter, the rake
scattered over their yard. That's not
his job, yet there he trawls and kicks
through maple leaves, his shuffle off
kilter, from what?—birth defect or stroke?—
and he's not even thirty.   The toys
he has to pinch against his hip with
knuckle-boned hand, fingers don't work,
the neighbors away, no one to help.
Then he climbs onboard that space capsule
full of noisy silence, engages blade,
and launches out into a green heaven
where grass becomes a sky swept clean.
Round and round so smooth—no hitch,
no stumble—the ship glides through
a swirling galaxy he orders,
shooting stars all tucked inside his shirt
for a moment.   Halfway through the flush
of leaves a metallic screech mows the air—
that toy he missed, a dozer
buried by the boy. The mowerman curses
and kicks the leaves to hold the toy
scissored into two.

Earth Diving

Ray needs no goggles,
no snorkel, no tank, no wetsuit
for his Boxer-Bull, all muscle, all focused self.
Besides, the goggles wouldn't work—
the cleft between his eyes
that's like a sliding board for my thumb
is too deep for such gear.
He swims these woods just fine
in his own fierce and goofy way,
chasing chipmunks and black bears,
following the currents of luxurious smells.

When Ray finds something good
like the slimy rot of a dead squirrel,
or the fresh green ooze of calf pie,
or his favorite—crawdad-inflected,
fish-scale glittered, neatly deposited
otter shit—he doesn't roll like most dogs,
he dives—head down, shoulder leading,
quick, again and again, the only way
to rub that odiferous joy
into just the right spot—
a smear from jowl to ear,
from cheek to neck,
a perfume no bottle can hold,
no towel can wipe away.

And why should my pal Jim
be yelling so much?
He need not be jealous.
I'd gladly share.

Mal and Slick's Ballad

"my adventrous Song
...intends to soar
Above th' Aonian Mount, while it pursues
Things unattempted yet in Prose or Rhime."
—Milton, *Paradise Lost*, Book 1

My name is Mal and this is Slick
have we got a tale to tell—
that book you read most every night
well it can go to hell. (Ha!)

The story you love, your Adam and Eve,
the tree no one could touch
was created by some faded men
who loved their power too much. (Ho!)

Why would a god so full of love
make such a tempting tree?
He knew for sure that fruit would go
on Eve's first shopping spree. (Hee!)

Take it, Slick.

> The garden there, the garden here,
> The garden in your head,
> The garden then, the garden now,
> That garden isn't dead.

One version says that Eve said no
two times before her yes.
She took it for its wisdom, see,
not its pretty dress. (Oh!)

That boy, her love, he couldn't wait
when offered this good fruit.
He chomped it down in one big bite
and then he got the boot. (Ow!)

The fig leaves came, the fig leaves went,
the fig leaves came again.
Another little snakey rose
to find a furry den. (Oo!)

Chomp it, Slick.

> The garden here, the garden there,
> The garden in your head,
> The garden then, the garden now,
> That garden isn't dead.

The boy, of course, he blamed his wife,
but no one moved *his* teeth,
and now I'm stuck inside his throat,
gulped each time he breathes. (Yuck!)

The girl, of course, she blamed poor Slick—
"He made me eat that fruit!"
Absurd, this trick, to blame my friend
and call him such a brute. (Yeah!)

Those faded men, they named me Malus
to put the blame on me.
How callous are them stem wankers
who cannot let us be. (Yo!)

Own it, Slick.

> The garden here, the garden there,
> The garden in your head,
> The garden now, the garden then,
> That garden isn't dead.

Religion is a sickness sure,
an opiate for the masses,
what better way to hold them down
then call them all fine asses. (Sup!)

Religion has to live on sin
to save us from ourselves,
but what if sickness is the model
for how to live in hell? (So!)

You call me Big, you call me rotten,
call me your iPads,
but you're the one with a loaded gun
aimed at your gonads. (Sa!)

You shit your house, you shit your sky
like it'll never matter,
but what's it like to turn the tap
and see your own piss water? (Yo!)

Oh, Joni-girl, you got it wrong
you can't go back to there,
just listen to my serpent friend
and untangle that big hair. (Ha!)

Take it, Slick.

     The garden there, the garden here
     The garden isn't dead.   (Not yet.)
     The garden then, the garden now
     The garden's in your head.   (That's right.)

Hawk Says Finally

Once in the gap between hills
Hawk hovered against
hard blue sky for so long—

no twitch no strain each
muscle twining with wind
red tail coppering the sun—

the blustering air turned
Hawk into a cluster of stars
a sudden constellation

outshining Orion and Bear
a new god to kneel to
in song and prayer.

When You Realize the Future

Pollen, like baby's breath,
clouds the air, a fine dust
of pine, chestnut, and oak.

At dusk, the same air swells
with quiet blinking
as lightning bugs
fire the dark.

Later a whippoorwill—
its beating song
a whisper
of a faraway
heart.

None answer
in reply.

The quiet
of the country woods
suddenly turns
empty and

Lincoln's Ax

at Abraham Lincoln Library and Museum, Harrogate, TN

Inside the lobby of the Lincoln Museum, a song sparrow flies from statue's head to thud against plate glass window. On the other side, clouds and vultures float in blue. Sparrow tries again, stays high, tapping glass with wings; below, people nibble cookies, drink, enjoy the reception—no panic in their trapped hearts, no urgency in their polite conversation and sunny smiles. Over all, young Lincoln lords from a giant stump, smooth face unbearded, eyes clear, hand atop hound's head, the other near an ax, marble white and innocent as his eyes were then. I stand at the door calling the song of the song sparrow over and over on my phone app, battery low, warning light red. Sparrow with a song that starts with three sharp notes replies to the recording, a duet of trapped voices. The door is never open wide enough.

I want that stone ax. I want to break the stone we call glass. I want a sparrow's emancipation. What would it cost if I shattered this wall? How would I make sure no shard struck me or the bird? And if I do *not* free this bird, what will that cost? Too much, I tell you, too much. The little deaths we daily leave behind accumulate with each step.

People leave, the lobby clears. The manager stays late. Sparrow has a spiderweb stuck to his tail. He is too tired, like Lincoln near the end, victory imminent and yet so much loss. I set the caller on the threshold and step back. Sparrow flits inches from freedom, but no closer. The caller has called in his mate. Sparrow flies down to mirror her pace, back and forth, a feather's width separates him from her tender, quiet preening. The battery dies, the tinny sound dissipates. The manager fills a bowl of water, scatters crumbs. She has to go. There's nothing more we can do. She locks the door, and we walk away.

It's just a common sparrow, I tell myself, a nickel's worth of fluff. His mate would not agree, I'm sure, nor would the young waiting in the nest. I walk to forget without luck, wondering about the other daily deaths we ignore, or never know we cause, or are utterly helpless to prevent.

Next morning, I find doors open and no sparrow. Hope turns shallow as the water bowl. I search museum with the manager, Lincoln heads watching as I *ssh-ssh* to flush the bird. Blankets of quiet pile up to weigh us down. Finally he emerges in a room where he flits under wooden table and chairs. I close the door, carry a large cloth—it's all we can find. Sparrow is slower now, weaker, but still elusive when I throw the sheet, his wings a shadow of escape. He lands high on a curtain, just out of reach. I climb a chair, snatch feathers from his chest. Nothing more. He is so tired he falls asleep in the thicket of table legs. The manager tries, slower, slipping cloth into place before flinging to capture a flutter—so tiny it looks like nothing more than a wrinkle. I cup wings, hold it tender, and hurry into sunshine. My hands open, the sheet unspreads. Sparrow flutters only a few feet, too exhausted for more. He wobbles in the grass, unsure of sun and once hard sky. I wonder if he will make it to see the night.

In caves nearby slaves slept before slipping through that narrow door in the mountain called Cumberland Gap. What freedom did they find? What exhaustion tagged them along the way? And now, what windows must we still strike and shatter? Borrow that ax. Sharpen it true. Sing your song. But do not wait.

The Oldest Spoon

The hoot owl lifts up the dark for all to taste.

> Your twitching hand
> keeps me awake.

> My body's heat
> scootches you away.

> To spoon
> is seldom easy.

In that hoot-owl dark, the Big Dipper is nothing but

> Once I glanced into
> where your parents slept

> on a narrow bed
> spooning for over fifty years.

> Their ashes now fill
> a single grave.

the oldest spoon pointing us home.

Broken Wing

The ghost of Dove
that shadow-dusts our window
(head turned, wings wide)
marks the impact of surprise.
Sometimes Dove flies away,
sometimes not—
either way, the boom of soft bone
packed against glass
sounds like pain.

And what of the sound
of loneliness, that deeper ache?
When Wren sings from fence
and none reply—
cat slinking away,
nest empty of mate and eggs—
what does Wren feel
in that bubble of his body?
Does he want just one
thorn-prick,
just a little more pain
to pop it all away?

And Barred Owl with broken wing,
what do you want?
Not this, an Earth Day Fair
with too many people,
too much light, too much heat.
School children touch
your wing, your head.
Eyes wide, you stress-pant,
swivel and launch to flail and dangle from your keeper's arm
before she can right you once more.
Your wing bones healed
crooked, so now to fly

means to veer
away from mouse.
And to live means to know
only cage
or the tether to your keeper's hand.
Would you rather veer into the wild
of starvation?
Do you wish
for another car
to this time
end it all?

Cup of Sun

In the cup of sun-
flower's back, water puddles
and wren takes her bath.

Gluteal Fold

I love that crease,
that fold of skin,
that wrinkle there
even at your birth—

how it curves with your roundness,
how it hinges with the hinge of your hip,
how it stretches when you bend,
how it connects your orbed softness
with your solid trunk.

Like everyone, you have two,
but even you can't really see
their silent beauty
like I do.

Blink

Cardinal lies on porch, beak open,
wings splayed, graceless and still.
Her mate calls from the yellowbells,
but she doesn't answer.

I cup my hands to hold her, this morning
bitter cold. Her beak glows a red
lit from within, and her tail pulses
with her heart. She looks right in-
to me, her eyes so black—the membrane
no longer a separation, no longer
anything but us.

        What does she see?
A world of trickery, where air
betrays with hardness, the sky
solid enough to kill,
and me, trying to unknow
my way back into the earth.
I shiver. We both blink.

My hands grow numb as I listen to her
partner sing from the frost-covered grass.
I imagine little flames traveling
my veins, blood brighter with whatever
heat and power my great-grandma could call
as she laid on hands and healed
other people, other birds. Did she
lay her hands on me, my ears
that ached through infancy?
She held me, that much I know.

        My fingers tingle
cold. I pray and breathe and stroke
the bird's soft cheek and hope

my hands aren't just stealing heat.
Come back, I whisper, *come back*.

Geese honk down the valley.
Wren can't stop chattering
as clouds filter the rising sun.

She blinks more, lifts her beak.
Her red crest peaks. I step away
from windows, hold her to the morning light.

Is it time? I ask. She turns
her head, looks out, and launches
her *yes*, the air once more soft
enough to fly through, honest
enough for love.

The Intimacy of Spoons

Knives with serrated edges, their solid singularity and sureness of purpose,

forks too with fang teeth
and slots of air,
their habit of piercing—

neither will ever know
the intimacy of spoons.

How they hold each other—
knees cupped, thighs touching,

the long curve of spine
soft against belly and chest,

the nuzzled narrow neck,
this ladle of bodies.

Slowly your breathing softens, falls
into that space of sleep

where you twitch in dreams
and I hold on.

Acknowledgments

Grateful acknowledgment to the following publications and editors for supporting this work, sometimes in different form.

Appalachian Heritage: "The Intimacy of Spoons"

Appalachian Journal: "A Boat Called *Kinfolks*" and "First Hard Frost"

Appalachian Places: "Cup of Sun," "Mort for Short," "The Oldest Spoon," and "Wrestling the Dead"

Artemis Journal: "Know the Trees, One by One" and "Vessel"

Cutleaf: "Good Dirt" and "Stress Test"

Ekphrastic Review: "Whale Light"

Northern Appalachian Review: "Every Person Deserves a Statue and Every Statue Deserves a Sledgehammer," "Exercise," and "Still Dark"

Peauxdunque Review: "Sighs"

Pine Mountain Sand & Gravel: "Because in the Village of Where," "Broken Wing," "The Collar," "Elegy for my Body," "Trenched," and "What Happens to Bulldozers in Heaven"

Reflections on the New River: New Essays, Poems and Personal Stories: "Because in the Village of Where"

Salvation South: "Why Birds?"

Southern Poetry Anthology, Volume IX, Virginia: "Blink," "First Hard Frost," "Lasts," "Tim Slack, the Fix-It Man," and "To Spoon the Dark"

Southern Voices Anthology: "Coyote Grace," "Gas," "James and Jim Ponder Enough," "Spoonbill," and "To Spoon"

Still: The Journal: "Diminished," "James and Jim Ponder Enough," and "Spangled"

Tampa Review: "Tim Slack, the Fix-It Man"

Upper New Review: "Earth Diving," "Hawk Says Finally," "Ode to a Basket," and "To Spoon"

Writers by the River: Reflections on 40+ Years of the Highland Summer Conference: "When You Realize the Future"

Writing the Land: Virginia: "What If We Learn at Last, but the Land Stops Forgiving?"

The line, "Our ground time here will be brief," on page 47 comes from Maxine Kumin's poem, "Our Ground Time Here Will Be Brief," *Maxine Kumin: Selected Poems*, 1960-1990 (W.W. Norton, 1997).

A writer might work in isolation much of the time, but never without a community. For the many people and creatures who have helped me and these poems along the way, I'm grateful. These include: Grace Toney Edwards, Theresa Burriss, Ricky Cox, JoAnn Asbury (in memoriam), Parks Lanier (who gave me the Big Dipper), and all the Highland Summer Conference teachers and students over the years; Matt Dunleavy, Rick Van Noy, Tim Poland, Rosemary Guruswamy, and the Radford University English department; Stuart Dischell, Jim Clark (in memoriam), Terry Kennedy, Holly Goddard Jones, and the University of North Carolina-Greensboro Creative Writing family; Dick Hague, Pauletta Hansel, Mike Henson, Jim Webb (in memoriam), Dana Wildsmith, Sherry Cook Stanforth, Ali Hintz, and the Southern Appalachian Writers Cooperative kinfolk; Rhonda Armstrong, Anna Harris Parker, and the Augusta University students and faculty; Darnell Arnoult, Denton Loving, Robert Gipe, Frank X Walker, Crystal Wilkinson, Nickole Brown, Doug Van Gundy, Jesse Graves, Amy Wright, Todd Davis, Cathryn Hankla, and the Mountain Heritage Literary Festival and Hindman Settlement School reunions; Pam Campbell, kind reader; Kim Davis and Linda Parsons, publisher and editor and friends; the many readers who have kept these words alive; librarians everywhere; my students and teachers who have given so much; my parents and siblings for years and years of encouragement; all the bees and bears, basswoods and beeches, bobcats and beavers, and of course, all the birds—the natural world that offers such sustenance; and Sarah, inspiration, reader, and best spooner.

About the Author

Jim Minick is the author or editor of eight books, including *Without Warning: The Tornado of Udall, Kansas* (nonfiction), *Fire Is Your Water* (novel), and *The Blueberry Years: A Memoir of Farm and Family*. His work has appeared in many publications, including *The New York Times*, *Poets & Writers*, *Oxford American*, *Orion*, *Shenandoah*, *Appalachian Journal*, *Wind*, and *The Sun*. He serves as co-editor of *Pine Mountain Sand & Gravel*.

www.ingramcontent.com/pod-product-compliance
Lightning Source LLC
Chambersburg PA
CBHW022013080426
42733CB00007B/591